Sam Helps Recycle

Judith Bauer Stamper

TeachingStrategies™ • Washington D.C.

For Teaching Strategies, Inc.
Publisher: Larry Bram
Editorial Director: Hilary Parrish Nelson
VP Curriculum and Assessment: Cate Heroman
Product Manager: Kai-leé Berke
Book Development Team: Sherrie Rudick and Jan Greenberg
Project Manager: Jo A. Wilson

For Q2AMedia
Editorial Director: Bonnie Dobkin
Editor and Curriculum Adviser: Suzanne Barchers
Program Manager: Gayatri Singh
Creative Director: Simmi Sikka
Project Manager: Santosh Vasudevan
Designers: Ritu Chopra & Shruti Aggarwal
Picture Researcher: Anita Gill

Picture Credits
t-top b-bottom c-center l-left r-right

Cover: Istockphoto, Mark Coffey/ Olga Lyubkina/Istockphoto, Roman Milert/123RF, Dreamstime, Ann Murie/Dreamstime, Dreamstime.

Back Cover: Olga Lyubkina/Istockphoto, Lisa A. Svara/Shutterstock.

Title Page: Carmen Martínez Banús/Istockphoto, Mark Coffey/Istockphoto.

Insides: Masterfile/Jupiter Images: 3t, Mark Coffey/Istockphoto: 3b, Roman Milert/123RF: 4l, Starblue/Dreamstime: 4r, Mark Coffey/Istockphoto: 5c, Dreamstime: 5bl, Ann Murie/Dreamstime: 5bc, Dreamstime: 5br, Olga Lyubkina/Istockphoto: 6c, Lisa A. Svara/Shutterstock: 6b, Dev Carr/Photolibrary: 7, Mike Clarke/istockphoto: 8, Photoalto/Photolibrary: 9t, Phil Date/123RF: 9b, Vadim Kozlovsky/Shutterstock: 10-11, Mark Coffey/Istockphoto: 11r, Gunnar Kullenberg/Photolibrary: 12t, Mark Coffey/Istockphoto: 12b, Masterfile: 13, J-C&D. Pratt/Photolibrary: 14t, Mark Coffey/ Istockphoto: 14b, Moreno Soppelsa/Dreamstime: 15, Liane Cary/Photolibrary: 16t, Karam Miri/123RF: 16b, Frances M Roberts/Photolibrary: 17, Leonid Shcheglov/Dreamstime: 18l, Mark Coffey/Istockphoto: 18r, Istockphoto: 19, Photodisc: 20t, Mark Coffey/Istockphoto: 20b, Creatas/Photolibrary: 21, Willeecole/Dreamstime: 22l, Philip Date/Fotolia: 22r, Jane Norton/Istockphoto: 23t, Dreamstime: 23c, Joan Coll Jcvstock/Dreamstime: 23b, Elliot Westacott/Shutterstock: 24l, ZlatkoKostic/Istockphoto: 24r.

Teaching Strategies, Inc.
P.O. Box 42243
Washington, DC 20015
www.TeachingStrategies.com

ISBN: 978-1-60617-138-7

Library of Congress Cataloging-in-Publication Data
Stamper, Judith Bauer.
  Sam helps recycle / Judith Bauer Stamper.
    p. cm.
  ISBN 978-1-60617-138-7
  1. Recycling (Waste, etc.)--Juvenile literature. I. Title.
  TD794.5.S69 2010
  363.72'82--dc22
                        2009037267

CPSIA tracking label information:
RR Donnelley, Shenzhen, China
Date of Production: July 2015
Cohort: Batch 4

Printed and bound in China

6 7 8 9 10	15
Printing	Year Printed

Hi! My name is Sam. I'm helping
Maya and her mom recycle our trash.

I hear Maya calling me now.
Got to go!

3

Some of our trash goes into garbage cans. The rest goes into recycling bins.

Maya has a big stack of newspapers ready. Wait a minute; I have to get that newspaper I hid behind the bushes. I'll add it to the stack.

Cans and glass bottles are next. We put them into a separate bin.

Hey, are they throwing away my dog food? No, it's okay. These cans are already empty.

Plastic goes into the last bin. I run to get a bottle I left in the yard. I don't want to litter.

When I come back, I get a surprise. My food bowl is in the recycling bin. Why are they throwing my bowl away?

Sniff!

Before I can save my bowl, Maya calls me to get into the car. She says we're going to the recycling center.

We're also bringing old batteries and unused paint. It's not safe to keep them around.

In some towns, sanitation workers pick up the trash on one day and recycling bins on another day. Where we live, we do our recycling ourselves.

Maya's mom starts the car. Here we go!

Maya's mom says that each person in the United States produces more than 4 pounds of garbage a day. That's enough to make more than 60,000 truckloads of trash!

I wonder…where does all that garbage go?

I soon find out. We drive by a huge landfill.
My nose can smell it a mile away!

Maya's mom tells us that a landfill is a deep hole
dug into the ground. It has a lining of clay and
plastic at the bottom. The lining keeps the rotting
garbage from leaking into the groundwater.

There are big bulldozers pushing
huge piles of garbage that have been
dumped at the landfill. The trucks
pack it down with their wide tires.

I've heard Maya say that there's just too much trash to put in landfills. That's why we have to recycle paper, plastic, cans, and bottles. All these things can be reused and turned into new things.

I'm glad that we're at the recycling center, but I'm still worried about my food bowl.

I watch while some people put their newspapers into a big container. Then Maya and her mom dump their newspapers.

My paper goes in, too!

A sanitation worker comes over to pet me. He tells Maya that recycling paper saves lots of trees—and lots of energy, too.

He explains that our recycled paper gets packed into big bales that go to a paper-recycling factory.

At the factory, the old paper is turned into pulp. Then it goes through a machine that turns out miles of new paper every day.

Yelp!

Next, Maya's mom adds our bottles and cans to a big pile. A front-end loader scoops them up and dumps them into the back of a truck.

It makes a horrible racket. I wish I could cover my ears.

The worker says that the bottles and cans will go to a sorting facility that separates the glass and the metal. Then they go to separate factories to be recycled.

At one factory, the glass bottles are crushed and melted into a liquid. Then the liquid glass is poured into molds to make new bottles and other products.

The cans are taken to a different place. Before they leave the sorting center, though, they are crushed together into bales. Then they are taken to a factory that recycles metal. Recycled cans are made into new cans that can be recycled all over again.

Maya's mom unloads the plastic last.
I see my food bowl sitting on top of the pile.

The worker tells us that plastic bottles take up a lot of space. In some landfills, they may never decompose or waste away. That's why it's really important to recycle plastic.

He says that the plastic is sent from the recycling center to a factory. First, the plastic is cleaned. Then it is chopped up into little pieces. Finally, it is melted down and made into new plastic products.

On our way home, I worry about my bowl, but I still feel good about recycling.

When I go into the house, I get a great surprise. Maya shows me my new red bowl. She points out the recycling symbol on the side as she fills it with food.

While I'm eating, Maya and her mom talk about other recycled products. Maya's notebook comes from recycled paper. Some clothes are made from recycled plastic. Even some playground surfaces are made from old tennis shoes and rubber tires!

After I finish my food, I head straight to my doggy bed for a nap.

Recycling is a lot of work… but it's worth it!